GALLIPOLI:
A SOLDIER'S STORY
FORGOTTEN PHOTOGRAPHS OF CONFLICT

BRIAN EASTWOOD

Gallipoli: A soldier's Story
Brian Eastwood

This edition Copyright © 2022 by Brian Eastwood

The right of the author to be identified as the author of this work
has been asserted in accordance with the
Copyright, Designs and Patents Act 1988.

All rights reserved.
No part of this publication may be reproduced, stored in a retrieval system, or transmitted, in any form or by any means, electronic, mechanical, photocopying, recording or otherwise, without the prior permission of the copyright owners.

ISBN 978-1-910779-95-8

Typeset by
Oxford eBooks Ltd.
www.oxford-ebooks.com

In memory of Brian Eastwood, our dearly loved husband, Dad, Poppa and Great Poppa.

THE ANZAC CRUCIBLE

MILLIONS OF WORDS have been written on the military debacle that was Gallipoli, the tragic First World War encounter forever immortalised in Anzac Day memorial services in Australia and New Zealand and as Gallipoli commemorations around the world.

Young men, and some older, from Great Britain and Ireland, Australia, New Zealand, France, Newfoundland and India fought against Turkish troops of the Ottoman Empire between 25 April 1915 and 9 January 1916, with the allied powers aiming to invade the Ottoman capital of Constantinople.

Eight months of fighting ended in their retreat. Behind the warring armies, 130,842 soldiers from both sides lay dead, and 262,014 were wounded for a total of 392,856 casualties. Many of the dead lie in unknown graves.

New Zealander Ernest Young was at Gallipoli, a dismounted member of the Otago Mounted Rifles regiment which had left its horses behind in Egypt to fight as infantry in the misconceived campaign. He was in fact one of four Young brothers who served in the wider war, with all returning home after the conflict.

Ernie as we will come to know him through these pages, had been

selected among 50 men chosen from the Otago Mounted Rifles to form a bodyguard for Sir Ian Hamilton, commander-in-chief of the ill-fated campaign. A smaller party of men drawn from this elite unit accompanied the general at all times.

He was with the escorting guard when the general inspected the men of the Australia, New Zealand Army Corps, the Anzacs who had landed at Cape Helles in May to support the British troops.

A soldier at the time was not permitted to have a camera, in case his capture, or just the enemy finding pictures, gave away positions and plans. But it seems Ernie's position as a bodyguard may have included a general officer's dispensation.

The wide coverage of the photographs he was able to take through a soldier's viewfinder suggests that he also helped escort Hamilton around many of the Anzac positions. Eventually Ernie asked to be returned to his own unit and was later wounded in the August attack at Hill 60.

His bandolier of 303 ammunition was struck near his right shoulder, exploding his right arm into oblivion. He was evacuated to England, surely 19 days of torment aboard a hospital ship.

In these pages, we are able to follow him as his wartime journey began with landfall from New Zealand in Egypt, through Gallipoli, recovery in England, and on the voyage home to New Zealand.

A family anecdote says after he arrived back in the Kaipara, he went to the banks of the Northern Wairoa River. There, he removed his prosthetic arm, picked up his rifle, and threw both into the muddy river waters.

Now a century after Gallipoli, a fading photograph album found in a drawer in a farmhouse at Waihue, known locally as 'Struggler's Gully', in the Kaipara District of New Zealand has opened the way for us to follow a soldier's journey through Gallipoli and beyond.

Daughter-in-law, Pat Young remembers, "Writing with his left hand was about the only thing he ever had any trouble with. He could even pull his motor mower to bits and put it together again. Using a wheelbarrow around the farm was simple he always said. He just tied the right handle with a rope that he put over his shoulder and around his back and waist."

Ernie grew up in Mosgiel, in New Zealand's Otago, where he started working life as a clerk for an electrical firm . When war came he joined 5th Otago Hussars and left on October 16,1914 with the First Expeditionary Force Main Body, on the ship Ruapehu, bound for Egypt. He was 28 years old when wounded at Gallipoli around August 21 1914 and he died in 1963, aged 75.

ZEITOUN CAMP

It must have seemed the war was starting as a pleasure cruise going halfway around the world and into the Mediterranean Sea. Leaving Auckland, New Zealand, in the first week of October 1914, the New Zealanders sailed around the south coast of Australia, called at Hobart in Tasmania, visited Fremantle on Australia's west coast, crossed the Indian Ocean to Capetown, and journeyed on north to what was then Ceylon before finding the Suez Canal and making landfall at Alexandria. It was the first day of December 1914. The soldiers were quickly sent by train to Zeitoun, a camp outside Cairo.

Training soon started for both the infantry and mounted rifle brigades. One soldier wrote home saying, 'General Godley is a great believer in hard work and plenty of it. We are drilling from morning until evening and sometimes we go out all night.'

But Christmas Day was spent quietly in camp with officers contributing a day's pay towards a Christmas dinner for the troops.

There were long route marches through and around Cairo. Leave was spent checking out their unfamiliar surroundings.

Some New Zealanders were called out to take part in the defence of the Suez Canal when Turkish forces attacked in January and February 1915. Many thought that they

would be off to Europe, perhaps in February, but it did not turn out that way. They did not know that they would soon land on the shores of Gallipoli and a date with destiny.

Reveille in the camp sounded at 5.30 every morning. The men paraded at 8.30am, trained until 2pm and arrived back at camp for dinner. After a short parade they were free for the day and because the camp was close to Cairo, the city became their playground.

The strange Egyptian dress fascinated the men from New Zealand and they noticed the contrast between fine buildings and poor native quarters, the well dressed successful citizens, and often diseased and blind people in the poorer areas.

But they enjoyed bargain hunting and the haggling. In their remarkable book *New Zealanders at War*, editors McLean and McGibbon quote Ernie's brother Bert's letter to his sister saying that Mosgiel boys were sending silk handkerchiefs home.

'Silk is very cheap here and labour is a long way cheaper. You can have a real good laugh if anybody shows you silk presents from Egypt and thinks them valuable. For God's sake don't let the cat out of the bag and tell anyone the paltry sum we are spending on them.'

EGYPT

MANY FOREIGN ARMIES have camped outside Cairo over the centuries. As did soldiers of the past, the New Zealanders wondered and puzzled over the pyramids and Sphinx. Zeitoun was just nine miles by tram to the monuments to an earlier civilisation and Sphinx, and easy to visit. A wartime visitor wrote, 'Surprisingly, the pyramids and Sphinx are on the edge of Cairo. If you turn your back on them you can see the residential city slums', a view that has not dramatically changed to this day.

DISPATCH RIDERS

IN THE BEST New Zealand 'do it yourself' tradition these dispatch riders have built their own bunker and hideaway. Many of them brought their own motorbikes to the war.

Troopers of the Mounted Rifles brought their own horses, but were paid for them by the government. The motor cyclists had no such compensation. They paid for maintenance themselves and were not even allowed to ride the bikes on their own trips in to town.

But judging by the ledge decorations behind the men they managed to find other pleasures. One man recorded that there were plenty of 'wet canteens' in Cairo and the beer was mostly good . . . of course some have bad beer but most of them get Edinburgh beer and that is far ahead of the local tack'.

The bunker in the photo was probably the company dispatch riders' headquarters, giving them a place to get a little relief from heat and sand. Especially sand.

Another letter told of their difficulties. 'Everything we have had to eat seemed to be stuffed with far more sand than sugar. If you could hear the boys saying grace before meals you would be sure the enemy was not shrapnel but sand. Sand! — in everything, on everything!'.

THIRST

IF EVERY PICTURE tells a story this one would probably say, 'Hot, dusty, dry and thirsty — and too many clothes!'

One of the soldiers in Egypt wrote home: 'Temperature here today is 100 degrees and not yet ten o'clock. The weather is getting simply unbearable and the flies are the absolute limit. They have driven the horses frantic.'

The photo could also tell of the strange creatures Ernie and his comrades had discovered in the Egyptian desert. Besides snakes and sand storms they met up with scorpions, described as 'like huge spiders, very poisonous dreadful creatures'.

And there were locusts. 'We have been practically smothered with them day after day. They fly in large droves perhaps covering twenty miles'.

Strange sights for New Zealanders but they had to deal with them 'in our tents, in our clothes, blankets, in the boiling tea, and they even cling to the manes of our horses'.

The men were sometimes sent out on marches with full war packs, complete with underclothing, towel, razor etc. An officer sick in his tent saw them arrive home one afternoon — 'the boys are just back covered in dust, sand and blinded with sweat.'

Soldiers wished they were gone from Egypt, but they could not have imagined what lay ahead for them on Gallipoli.

DRESSING STATION — CAIRO

MOST WARTIME DRESSING stations were just a few miles behind the lines. This one was a permanent base in Cairo probably in front of the New Zealand hospital at Pont de Koubbeh.

In Ernie's photo taken before he left for Gallipoli, these men do not appear to be wounded but are probably some of the sick. Illness and infection was a continuing problem in the primitive confines of camp.

But considering the events of those times and the heat of the Egyptian desert, the troops were said to be in good health. The men in the queue are possibly out-patients living in a nearby army camp. Dressing stations were later known as casualty clearing stations and were usually near or beside a railway line. They were the first static and well-equipped medical centre a wounded man would arrive at after he was taken from the battlefield. It was where triage decisions were made about the soldier's future. If his wounds were considered survivable he could be patched up and sent back to his unit or sent on to a base hospital.

Typically a casualty clearing station could have as many as 1,000 patients at one time. Some urgent surgery, including amputations, was often done there. But sadly the site of a World War One clearing station is today often the site of a large military cemetery.

HOSPITAL — CAIRO

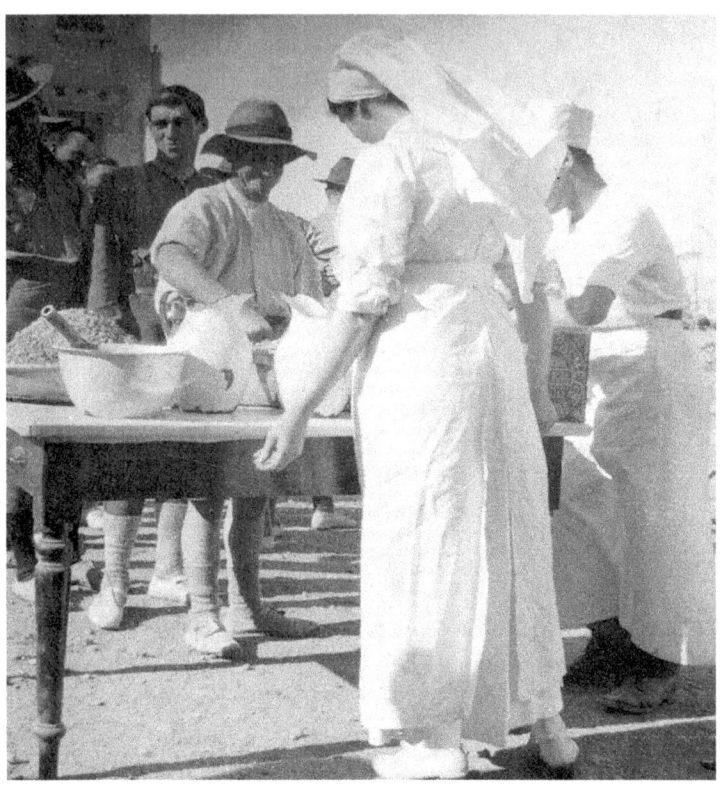

By July 1915 there were two hospitals in Egypt for New Zealand soldiers. Number 1 New Zealand Hospital was at Port Said while the other, near Cairo at Pont de Koubbeh, was a two-storied stone building lent by the British commander of the Egyptian Army for the use of sick and wounded New Zealand soldiers, staffed by British and New Zealand medical corps, including 25 New Zealand nurses. New Zealand Stationary Hospital Number 2 arrived in July to take over Pont de Koubbeh.

They were badly needed. It was recorded that some men arrived during August with their wounds septic and wearing the original dressing that had been applied in the battle at Gallipoli.

Ernie, wounded on August 21, was more fortunate and was in England within nineteen days.

Later, New Zealand Hospital Number 2 was relocated to England and renamed Number 1 New Zealand General Hospital.

PONT DE KOUBBEH HOSPITAL

ERNIE PROBABLY TOOK this photo of Pont de Koubbeh hospital just days before heading off to Gallipoli about April 10, 1915. Until then little had been done to take care of wounded New Zealand soldiers in their own hospitals and they had been taken into Australian and British hands.

Twenty-five New Zealand Army nurses were first to serve at Pont De Koubbeh. A large two-storied building with deep verandahs, it could accommodate 250 men when taken over but marquees were erected in the large quadrangle to increase the bed numbers to 500.

Ernie was wounded on August 22 and records show he was transferred straight to the hospital ship Franconia on the same day.

After a quick voyage to England he was admitted to St Thomas hospital in London on September 10. He had the good fortune to be under the best treatment just 19 days after being hit.

GALLIPOLI:
QUINN'S POST

As TIME WENT on Quinn's became more organised and comfortable, especially after it was handed over to the popular Colonel William Malone and his Wellington Battalion to sort out. On May 29 they were shifted after eight days' action on Courtenay's Post to take over Quinn's.

Writing home to the Taranaki Daily News, Malone described the situation there.

'It was in a parlous condition and a source of anxiety to army commanders. The frontage of the post is about 200 yards. The men expect to be blown off the edge of the cliff on which it rests. It was a dilapidated, demoralized and filthy hole. But all it wanted was cleaning, repairing, reorganizing, rearming and the cultivation of domestic virtues.

'Within one week of taking over my men got all over the Turks; shot and bombed them. Within eight days we settled the Turks and practically turned hell into heaven, an achievement as great as that of any battalion. In four weeks we fired 16 mines, threw say 5,600 bombs and got thrown at us, say 200. Our casualties too were very small. Of this I am prouder than of anything.'

BOMB-PROOF SHELTERS

QUINN'S POST BECAME a household name in New Zealand and Australia after the Anzacs landed at Gallipoli on April 25, 1915. It was named after Australian Captain Quinn of their 15th battalion. Later promoted to Major, he was killed in an early morning attack on the enemy. It became the place of some very heavy fighting for the Australians and the New Zealanders.

One day after the landing they were on a ridge a little more than one kilometre from the beach and very close to the Turkish enemy. Although estimates varied a little, most reckoned that some Anzac and Turkish trenches were no more than three metres apart around Quinn's.

From the afternoon of the 26th the ridge was the point of incessant attack from the Turks.

The front line was on top of this hill and described by one soldier as a small plateau.

Because they were so close the weapons used were usually hand grenades and trench mortars. Sapper J. McKenzie wrote: 'Both sides fill in time and make the night hideous by throwing one another presents of high explosives.'

QUINN'S POST — MILE TRACK

QUINN'S WAS ESTABLISHED in the first days after the Anzac landing after a few New Zealanders had advanced across Mule Valley to the next ridge. A huge Turkish attack sent them back to a ridge on the opposite side of the valley where they hung on below a commanding knoll with little cover. The New Zealanders started to make a track to the top using the cover of a small dry creek. Australians came to help work the track up further and establish a position that would enter the history books of the conflict.

In the beginning just getting to Quinn's could be fatal. As well as bursting shells spraying shrapnel around, there were Turkish snipers scattered around the slopes, hiding in bushes and scrub.

The approach was named Shrapnel Point and Death Valley — labels that told their own tale. Later the area was renamed Monash Valley.

But after a few weeks it was no longer such a danger. One soldier wrote home in June, 'Huge barricades of sandbags were built up as a protection against cross-fire. A deep sap or track was cut around the hillside and now we go up and down in safety'.

On the left of Ernie's photo can be seen the barricade of sandbags running up from Death Valley.

To go up to Quinn's Post during the first days after the landing at Anzac Cove meant making a

MAIN APPROACH

dangerous journey, but official war correspondent, Malcolm Ross told his readers in September 1915, 'You approach it now through long communication trenches leading over a hill and up what is known as Monash Valley, formerly known as Shrapnel Valley. In places you still have to dodge an occasional sniper's bullet and yesterday you were lucky if you got through the shrapnel unhit.'

A month later another newspaper man wrote: 'Once in the early days the way to Quinn's was through a hail of bullets, up a hill, down into a valley, with the enemy peering down from the top.' But now he found it, 'no longer a matter of extreme peril coming up the valley, for there was a sap most of the way.'

That way looks safe in Ernie's photo of the virtual sandbag fortress. It also gives an idea of the huge number of bags that were filled during the campaign over the whole peninsula.

The men Ernie photographed look tired but it would have been a task they carried out as quickly as they could. The first layers along the tracks were presumably filled and stacked at night. At times there may have been more hard labour than hard fighting.

SANDBAG WORK

ERNIE SEEMS TO have taken this photo in the early days of Quinn's Post. The sandbagged stronghold was a haven for any soldier after a time in the front line at the top of the hill.

Much danger came from exploding shells with flying shrapnel coming from all directions. Sandbags turned dugouts into places that were safer than being in a trench. Even so, the troops complained that for them, going back for a 'rest' really meant filling sandbags.

An artillery officer calculated that 'a mile of trench required perhaps 100,000 bags'. Approximately 2,000 sandbags were needed to make a gun battery protected enough for the men and gun.

The Anzacs at the Dardanelles mostly stayed in one place, but if they did advance or retreat they couldn't take the bags with them to the new positions.

Having enough bags to fill was a continuing problem and urgent requests were made home to New Zealand for more of the 33 inches long and 14 inches wide jute bags.

An advertisement in the New Zealand Herald in November 1915 read: 'The Newmarket Methodist School will be open each day and evening next week for the making of sandbags for the use of soldiers at Gallipoli.

An invitation to assist is extended to all who wish to do so.

MUD SHOOT

WHILE MODERN MACHINE guns were being used on the warring enemies on Gallipoli, other means of attack were needed. Making bombs from tin cans was a popular sideline for the Anzacs. The timing and throwing of them became an art, with former cricket players being called in as expert bomb throwers.

But since it was costly to attack above ground, both sides tried to work underground. Tunnelling became an important part of the effort to win battles. The idea was to tunnel under the enemy trench and plant mines to blow up just before a big attack.

Coal miners and engineers among the troops were roped in to do the work. One soldier told how they had miles and miles of tunnels, drives and listening galleries. It was dangerous work and often the men heard the Turks digging their tunnels coming the opposite way.

After the war a visitor to Gallipoli wrote: 'Many of the tunnels which were dug in the area between Lone Pine, Courtney's Post and Steele's Post are collapsing, which makes it possible to see how thickly honeycombed with tunnels this part of the battlefield was.'

The dirt from the tunnels was needed to fill sandbags and an ingenious way to shift it quickly downhill was by a smooth wooden mud shoot, as Ernie saw these men doing.

CANTERBURY GULLY

CANTERBURY GULLY WAS just below Walker's Ridge, lying on the New Zealander's main path to the front line and the track can be seen winding along the gully floor. Canterbury Mounted Rifles were operating in this area for much of the Dardanelles' campaign.

The Canterbury men did not land with the first troops at Anzac Cove on April 25 but stayed in Egypt until May 5 to finish training. When they were ordered to Gallipoli they went not as mounted troops but as infantry. Except for a few officers' mounts and some draught horses for transport work, their horses were left in Egypt. Twenty five officers and 451 other ranks sailed from Alexandria on May 9 aboard HMT Grantully Castle to arrive at Anzac Cove.

Just four days later they were sent straight into the front line on Walker's Ridge.

One hundred years later in his book *Gallipoli, The Battlefield Guide*, author Mat McLachlan noted that 16 men of the Canterbury Mounted Rifles remain here in this area in one of the smallest interments on Gallipoli — Canterbury Cemetery.

In a now almost forgotten sideshow away from the Anzac's main area, the New Zealand Infantry Brigade, together with the 2nd Australian Infantry Brigade, were taken by the Royal Navy to Cape Helles on the

WOUNDED, CAPE HELLES

very southern tip of the Dardanelles Peninsula.

The idea was to support British troops in an attack on Krithia, a village that was meant to be taken in the first few days.

At 10.30 am on May 7 the action started in broad daylight. Wellington Battalion was on the left, Auckland in the centre and Canterbury on the right, with Ernie's Otago Battalion held in reserve. They advanced across rough ground to reach the British soldiers.

Next day they attacked over 100 yards of flat paddock resulting in many casualties among the New Zealanders under fire from Turkish machine guns. Because of the flowers that later grew there it is known as the Daisy Patch.

Orders came from British General Hunter-Weston to attack again in the afternoon but with the same result. The futile attack finally faded out in the late afternoon and the village was not captured.

In the end it was a consolation to have gained 500 valuable yards because it meant shelter in the gullies where the wounded could be treated, as Ernie's photo shows.

New Zealanders were withdrawn but by then had suffered an awful total of 771 casualties.

WATER FATIGUE

In a military campaign that is now remembered for poor planning as well as extreme hardship, the failure to provide sufficient water for men and animals on Gallipoli had unfortunate results.

Keith Murdoch, reporter on the peninsula and father of future media mogul Rupert Murdoch, wrote to the Australian Prime Minister: 'We have about 105,000 men on the peninsula — flies are spreading dysentery at an alarming rate and the sick rate would astonish you. It cannot be less than 600 a day.'

Water was needed for personal hygiene as well as drinking water. Some men were able to swim at the beach although that was sometimes stopped by Turkish snipers and flying shrapnel. Authorities never imagined that the troops would be stalled in the heights for eight months, but there is no water on a mountainous ridge. After the war a Gallipoli Commission found that British General Frederick Stopford and his staff were partly responsible for the lack of water for the soldiers.

Famous Australian newspaper man Charles Bean complained: 'We only have two old water pontoons for all the men but one single storm would finish them off.' In fact they both sank in June.

Water fatigue involved walking perhaps a mile down to the beach, filling two canisters and returning up the stairs and steep slopes to the lines.

By the beginning of July wells had been dug in Shrapnel Gully but it meant a long wait for a turn to fill the cans.

TRENCH — WALKER'S RIDGE

It is said that every picture tells a story and this one shows the reality of dirty, cramped conditions and the discomfort of a front line trench. The face of the young soldier in the forefront tells of his exhaustion.

Judging by the photo, Ernie himself was either lying down or kneeling when he was in the trench. It was not a good idea to put your head above the parapet.

Not as well remembered as positions such as Quinn's Post, it was essential to hold Walker's Ridge to prevent the Turkish infantry coming down from the north and sniping from hills overlooking Monash Valley and Shrapnel Gully.

Walker's Ridge was the first place the New Zealanders dug in after the landing at Anzac Cove. Enemy attacks couldn't shift them from the ridge and some of their defending troops remained there, on the north-west left of the front line, until the day of the evacuation in December.

The ridge was named for British Brigadier-General H B Walker, a leader well thought of by the colonials.

Next ridge along was named Russell's Top, the position where New Zealander Major-General Andrew Russell had his headquarters.

There was one wholly Australian Division on Gallipoli together with the combined Australian and New Zealand Division — the Anzacs.

SALT LAKE — SUVLA

THE VIEW FROM this ridge, known as the Apex, gives an idea of the steep land fought over by the Anzacs at Gallipoli.

In the distance, about eight kilometres to the north, can be seen Salt Lake. Almost dry, it drains into Suvla Bay, the scene of a well planned landing but poorly executed advance by British forces.

Their plan was to head south and link up with the Anzacs to help take the high ground of the almost 1,000 feet Sari Bair range. They never arrived.

Down to the left is Chailak Dere the valley that the New Zealanders fought their way up in the dark on August 6, 1915. To make it a complete surprise they carried only bayonets and advanced without bullets in their rifles. It was on August 8 from this ridge that the never to be forgotten attack began on the summit of Chunuk Bair, just half a kilometre further up the hill from here.

In May 1925 at the opening of Chunuk Bair Memorial, General Godley, the commander of the Anzac Division, told the 400 strong crowd: 'It was here (the Apex) that the gallant Colonel Bauchop fell at the head of his regiment, the Otago Mounted Rifles'.

Ernie Young would have taken part. He took this photo sometime between the 10th and 21st August, the day that he was seriously wounded in the attack on Hill 60.

MONASH GULLY

THESE TWO SOLDIERS seem quite happy as they stroll down Monash Gully, apparently feeling safe when Ernie took their photo.

Called Shrapnel Valley at the coast end, the top part of the valley near the front line was named Monash Gully after the Australian commander, General Sir John Monash, considered one of the top First World war commanders.

In the first days ashore the Australians suffered huge losses in this valley. Some newspaper reports told of the unbelievable loss of 30 to 40 men a day from sniper fire in the Monash area. Enemy snipers watched for any movement from the top of the hills above the gully.

Their hideouts were fittingly dubbed 'Dead Man's Ridge' and 'The Bloody Angle' by the soldiers who had to endure the hike up to the front line.

The gully needed to be made safe because it was the main thoroughfare for the Anzacs making their way to places such as Quinn's, Courtney's and Steele's Posts.

When the New Zealanders arrived they sent several parties of two sharpshooters each, to watch and deal with enemy sniper's nests. Eventually they made it safe.

Later the way was made even safer at the top end of the valley with a path lined with walls of sandbags.

LOOKING UP TO COURTNEY'S POST

SITTING BETWEEN QUINN'S and Steele's Posts on the Anzac's front line ridge seen in the distance, Courtney's Post was named after Lieutenant Colonel Richard Courtney, commander of Australia's 14th Battalion. Courtney's trenches were dug two days after the Anzac landings and were never lost.

At midnight on May 18, Turks attacked in great numbers, their first effort mostly against Courtney's Post. It was here that legendary Australian soldier, Corporal Albert Jacka, won the Victoria Cross.

After the May battles, Wellington Infantry Battalion took over Courtney's Post with Lieutenant Colonel William Malone in command. They took turns every eight days with Otago Infantry Battalion, but Malone stayed through that time as commander for both units.

He made improvements, repairing earthworks and setting up a sniper's group to gain the upper hand over no-man's-land. Courtney's Post overlooked the Turkish positions.

In The Troopers' Tale, a history of Otago Mounted Rifles it was noted that 'O.M.R suffered fewer casualties than most other Anzac units because their normal location was at rugged outposts where little fighting took place.'

Except that during the August campaign at Bauchop's Hill and at Hill 60, where Ernie was hit, the regiment took big losses. Their eventual total on Gallipoli was reckoned to be 130 dead and 269 wounded.

SHRAPNEL GULLY

AMONG ALL THE confusing hills, valleys, cliffs and canyons on the shore in front of Anzac Cove there was one that soon earned itself a nickname. In the first days Shrapnel Gully was a very dangerous place to walk but the easiest way to the Anzac front line from the beach and used by many.

The Turks soon realised that it was an easy target. A letter from a Gallipoli soldier told how 'they never cease to sweep it with a shower of shell. It is easy to understand how its present title was suggested'. Shrapnel falling into the gully was said to make a curious whistling noise.

Sapper Ion Idriess, Australian author and former soldier who served as a spotter for famous sniper Billy Sing, remembered in his book *The Desert Column* based on his Gallipoli and Egyptian experiences: 'The Turks have a special trench filled with expert snipers — unerring shots who have killed God only knows how many of our men coming along this road'.

But later, 'A splendid track has been cut by Australian and New Zealand engineers from the beach right into Shrapnel Gully and the journey that on the first terrible night was punctuated with lives of men, can now be made with little inconvenience'.

A tell-tale fact is that the Shrapnel Valley Cemetery on Gallipoli was started soon after the landings and became the biggest to be used during the battles.

SAP TO NUMBER 2 OUTPOST

Two OUTPOSTS GUARDED the top end of North Beach at the most northern point of the Anzac front line. At the end of May, Ernie's regiment took over the positions of Outpost 1 and 2 from Canterbury Infantry Battalion that had dug in there during the first week after the landings.

The 540 men of Otago Regiment, including the bodyguard force of which Ernie was a member, were all together again. They were now to be used as infantry without their horses.

The outposts were approached by walking up the beach from Anzac Cove and climbing up a steep hillside. As with most parts of the landing beaches it was a dangerous walk to make in the day time and because of Turkish snipers was only made after dark. It was not long before their kilometre track was made a lot safer with a long sap, or trench, strengthened with sand bags.

Outpost Number 2 later became headquarters for Anzac commander Major General Alexander Godley, as well as the 16th Casualty Clearing Station, the Dental Unit, and the source of much needed water from a well found there. From here the climb began to gain the heights of the Apex for the start of the attack on Chunuk Bair.

Now Number 2 Outpost is the site of a cemetery with thirteen New Zealanders said to be buried there, although of 183 graves a total of 150 are of soldiers unknown.

SHELL BURSTING AT STEEL'S POST

ARGUABLY, THE MOST dangerous places to be in Anzac zone on Gallipoli were the three positions sitting on the ridges above Monash Valley. Quinn's was the most northern with Courtney's and Steel's in a line to the south-west. Ernie probably took this photo from the valley.

Each ridge was gained by a climb up a steeply angled cliff. A New Zealand newspaper reporter stood on Chunuk Bair in 1935, looked down to the beach, and wondered 'how the gallant Dominion troops ever reached their goal, the country being so rough and the approaches almost perpendicular'.

Men had to dig in as best they could in the rough ground at Steel's. The ridge was reached on the first day but the soldiers were still there in the middle of December when the evacuation got underway.

A visitor to the post in November 1915 wrote: 'Rifle fire continues as furiously as ever but the big gun bombardment has eased. The Turks seem afraid to go to sleep. Their whole front keeps pouring bullets on to our parapets during the dark hours.

A rescue party crept over Steele's parapet a few hours ago and brought in the nearest bodies of their comrades. Still some hundreds lie outside, a few right in front of the Turkish trench'.

MAIL DAY

Troops on Gallipoli were always eager for news from home. Anzac commander General Godley summed it up in 'thank you' letters to editors of the Taranaki Daily News, and the Auckland Weekly News. He wrote:

> Headquarters Australian and New Zealand Division Anzac Cove, Gallipoli.
>
> Dear Sir,
>
> On behalf of the New Zealand Expeditionary Force I wish to thank you very sincerely for your generosity in sending us the liberal supply of your excellent paper, which comes to hand regularly. We all enjoy the New Zealand news very much before passing it on.
>
> 'A mail from New Zealand is really a red letter day for us and everyone is cheered up when it comes to hand. To see New Zealand mail sorted on the hills of Gallipoli Peninsula is a sight to be remembered. It is four weeks today since we landed. There is practically no sickness among the troops who are all in excellent spirits.
>
> Yours very truly,
>
> A J Godley, Major-General, Commanding NZ Expeditionary Force'.

BURYING THE DEAD

THE HORROR AND absolute futility of war was never better demonstrated than by a truce to bury the dead arranged between 7.00am and 4.30pm on May 24, 1915 at Gallipoli.

Five days earlier, Turkish forces carried out a major assault on Anzac positions.

An Australian soldier likened it to a 'wallaby drive'. An estimated 42,000 soldiers attacked at around 3am and by mid-morning approximately 3,000 Turks lay dead and another 7000 were wounded. The Anzac dead totalled 160 with 468 wounded.

Newspaper correspondent Charles Bean wrote, 'Dead and wounded lay everywhere in hundreds. No sound came from that terrible space'. A British officer attached to the Anzacs found the scene 'indescribable'. He remembered that so awful was the stench that a Turkish officer gave him antiseptic wool to hold over his nose.

By the afternoon of that armistice day, the job of burying the dead was done. It was then that the enemies swapped cigarettes and smiled and talked as best they could with each other.

One soldier discovered 'that the Turks do not seem to be a bad sort of chap after all.' By five o'clock the two sides were shooting at each other again.

With his secret camera Ernie took a quick photo of the burying parties. Doubtless he would remember the sights and the stench of that day for the rest of his life.

ENGLAND:
ST THOMAS HOSPITAL

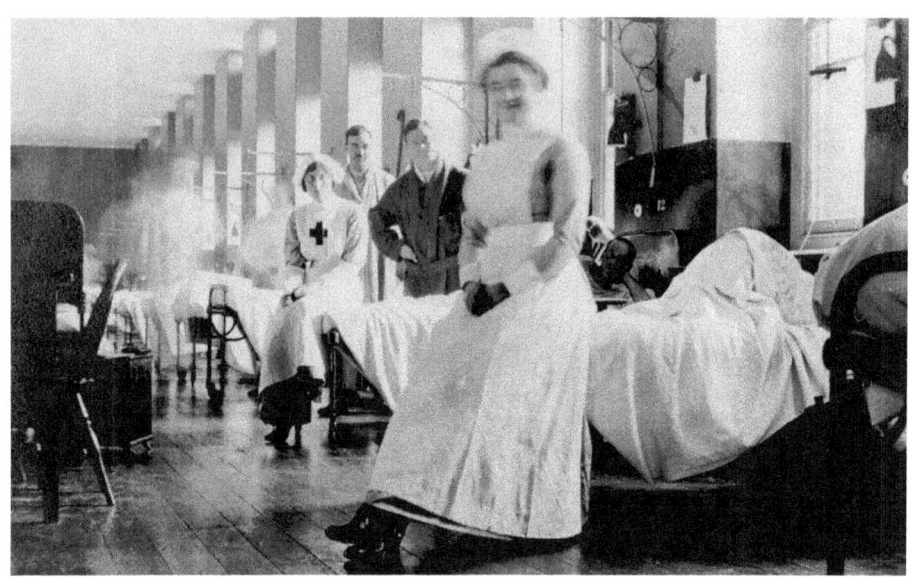

ALTHOUGH ERNIE THOUGHT that he had been wounded at Gallipoli on August 20, 1915 official records state that he was actually hit the next day. It was the start of the last big assault of the campaign, now known as the Battle of Hill 60.

Together with the Canterbury Mounted Rifles, 100 men from the Maori Contingent, Australian and British troops, the Otago Mounted Rifles attacked for 800 metres across an open valley. Ernie was one of the 60% of casualties who suffered that afternoon. Luck was with him and after he had nursed his mangled right arm down to the beach, he was in time to be taken aboard hospital ship Franconia heading for England. Nineteen days later he was safe in St Thomas Hospital, London.

Famous as the teaching hospital of the Florence Nightingale Nursing School, two hundred beds were set aside at the start of World War One as a military hospital for sick and wounded soldiers

After a stay of three months at St Thomas Hospital Ernie was transferred to the City of London Red Cross Hospital in Finsbury Square. He recovered quickly after the operation and someone wrote in his diary for him on New Year's Day 1916, 'In bed after operation'. That was followed by an entry that said, 'New Year party and tea'.

Four days later: 'Up in the afternoon. Wound healing fine' and next day 'Out for a walk'. Incredibly, after just another three days, he visited the British Museum, rode the underground and travelled in a bus. It seems as if he was a hard man to hold down and in a hurry to see all that London had to offer.

Transferred as an outpatient to Roehampton Hospital, Ernie stayed there for two months before going on to Base Depot at Hornchurch.

Granted sick furlough in April he set out to see as much of England and Scotland as he could.

In the photo Ernie is sitting fourth from the left with some of his comrades.

RIVER THAMES

When wounded and sick New Zealand soldiers came flooding back to England from Gallipoli in 1915 it was decided to open a London hospital especially for them.

The Mt. Felix estate in Walton-on-Thames had been taken over and was used by wounded British troops until June 1915 when they were moved out and the hospital was offered to the New Zealand War Contingent Association in England.

It was officially opened by the New Zealand High Commissioner in London, Sir Thomas McKenzie on August 2, 1915.

The property of 18 acres was just 15 miles from the London city centre. There were beautiful grounds with gardens, flower beds, grassy areas and fine old trees. It was enclosed by a brick wall, with one side running down to the Thames River so that boating became a popular pastime for convalescing servicemen.

In her book *Nursing in New Zealand, History and Reminiscences*, Hester Maclean wrote: 'It was with joy that New Zealand soldiers found themselves in a hospital run by their own countrymen and women. Here, when convalescing, they had many recreations, boating, swimming and watching the river with its interesting procession of boats passing up and down'.

Ernie Young seated on the left, is enjoying his peaceful day on the river.

EXPECTATION

WOUNDED OR SICK New Zealand soldiers arriving at an English hospital from Gallipoli, the Middle East or the Western Front, were visited straight away by someone from the New Zealand High Commissioner's office.

Both High Commissioner Sir Thomas McKenzie and Lord Plunket, a former Governor General of New Zealand, were active in the New Zealand War Contingent Association that looked after troops invalided to England.

Soldiers were not left to fend for themselves when discharged from hospital. They were directed to entertainment but also provided with places to spend their leisure time. Volunteer ladies, many with some connection to New Zealand, opened a restaurant in London's Victoria Street where the recuperating men could enjoy a chat, read or write home.

A London hostel was provided for them as a place to stay in the city. Supplied rent free by the British Government it was named the King George and Queen Mary Hostel. London police were instructed to take lost New Zealanders, or those in trouble, straight to the hostel. None were turned away from the house that could hold 400 men.

Those on leave were paid all the wages due to them and given free rail passes to any place in Great Britain that they would like to visit.

Or they could head off on their own adventures if they wanted to, as the three in this photo seem about to do.

NURSES OFF DUTY

LIFE WAS NOT at all easy for New Zealand nurses serving in the First World War. The work was hard and it could be dangerous. Many served on hospital ships going to and from Gallipoli, Egypt, Malta, Gibraltar and England.

On October 23, 1915 there were 36 New Zealand nurses heading for Greece from Egypt aboard the troop transport Marquette. Ten of them were drowned when the ship was torpedoed.

Sisters Harris and Philpotts told of a trip in convoy from New York to England, dodging submarines and arriving in London during an air raid.

At Walton-on-Thames hospital Sister Cutforth wrote that she was on night duty with Sister Morgan 'in a ward of seventy-one, some in a tent.

They are all cot cases so keep two nurses and one probationer very busy'.

A house at Sandwich, loaned by Englishman Major Waldorf Astor MP, was one of several homes used by New Zealand nurses to rest and recuperate when their own health had suffered from caring for the sick and wounded.

In off duty hours, time was sometimes spent by the nurses showing patients the sights of London.

Ernie Young kept a small diary written with difficulty because he had lost his right writing arm. Leaving his bed on January 2, 1916 after the operation to repair his wounds, it didn't take him long to start getting around. On January 10 he wrote: 'For morning tea at Strand Corner House with nurses'.

There was much more to see in England's capital city.

Although some nurses from New Zealand's soldier hospitals in First World War England liked to head for the city when on rest leave, at other times they enjoyed the countryside.

Sister Wilkin told how in June 1916: 'We brought a shipload of sick boys home to England and we then enjoyed nine bewildering days in what must be the most wonderful city in the world: London. We stayed in a hostel for sisters, kept by English ladies for stray nurses in London and were delighted with the kindness we received'.

Sister Lodge wrote of a five-day visit to London. 'Theatre tickets were provided for us each evening but sometimes we were much too tired to go after sightseeing all day'. Then came five days in the country as a guest at Lord Desborough's home, Taplow Court.

'At 11am each morning we were

rowed on the river, returned about 1pm. How we did love wandering through the woods along the river bank. The estate reaches a mile and a half along the river bank. We left by train from Whalley after a never to be forgotten ten-day holiday. It was there that we learned of Lord Kitchener's sad end'.

On June 13, 1916 Ernie Young was visiting London and also noted in his diary: 'Saw King and Queen drive from Buckingham Palace to St Paul's for memorial service for Kitchener'.

By September 1916 there were 357 New Zealand nurses on active service. It was soon realised that there was an obvious need for some rest and relaxation for the hard working ladies.

A generous offer gave them a home in Sandwich near Sheerness at the mouth of Thames River.

Whenever they had leave, some took the chance to head for London to do a little sightseeing.

Auckland siblings M and C Campbell, recently off the hospital ship Maheno and attached to Colchester Military Hospital, were given nine days' leave and they spent their time looking around London. A letter written by Sister Margaret Nixon told how after arriving in England she was 'very tired and worn out after my hard

ANZACS AT HAMPSTEAD

work in Egypt and Mesopotamia'.

She was then sent to Lady Desborough's place in Buckinghamshire where tired nurses were looked after and there she spent every minute in the garden and on the river. She wrote: 'I was very happy to be with New Zealanders again'.

The feeling was mutual. A wounded New Zealand soldier in the Walton-on-Thames hospital wrote in 1915:

'Our nurses are New Zealand's best, and even though we have been exceptionally lucky with all the nurses we have been under so far, we are more than satisfied to be under the care of our 'own girls' once more'.

London was a magnet for wounded New Zealand soldiers. Hampstead Heath, just six kilometres from Trafalgar Square in the middle of the city, was a popular place for convalescing Kiwis to spend time.

Perhaps trying to get fit again, Ernie started walking not long after leaving hospital. On February 8, 1915 his diary entry reads: 'To Hampstead Heath and had a good walk'.

An Auckland Star newspaper correspondent paid the heath a visit on August Bank Holiday weekend in 1915. He wrote of 'happy bands of youths and

AT ROEHAMPTON

maidens with khaki mostly as the masculine wear.

Anzac soldiers were there in force with no shortage of escorts in muslin'.

In spite of petrol shortages local people provided the recovering patients with plenty of transport. He saw 'motor cars, sidecars and charabancs' bringing the Kiwi boys to the park for their Sunday outing. With the big trees, plenty of wild life and wide open, grassy spaces Hampstead Heath must have seemed like a touch of home for the colonial lads.

London was full of New Zealanders the reporter noted. Noticeable with their colourful 'lemon squeezer hats of which they were very careful', it was said that there were always some New Zealanders standing on St Paul's Cathedral steps and always some leaning on the parapet of Westminster Bridge.

Ernie missed out on a white Christmas by just a few weeks while in Great Britain recuperating from the loss of his right arm. Until then a patient in St Thomas Hospital, he noted in his diary on February 15: 'Discharged from hospital for six days furlough'.

He made the most of his time. That evening he had dinner and tea out with friends before leaving a little before midnight on a train for Scotland.

Meeting up there with comrades, Ernie was taken to visit the Fairfield ship building yards to see eight submarines, six destroyers and the Dreadnought HMS Avenger being built.

After five interesting days looking around Glasgow he arrived back in London to be transferred to Roehampton Hospital. And if Christmas had passed, the snow had not.

His diary reads: 'Overhauled by a doctor and put on to massage'.

The next day Wednesday February 23: 'Weather cold and snowing'. Each day he wrote 'snowing hard' and 'still snowing'. On Saturday, 'Ground white with about four inches of snow'.

In the photo Ernie is standing at the back on the right and with his usual high spirits is pretending to hold hands with the worried looking young New Zealander alongside him.

Others in the photo may not be too happy with the cold weather but for a man from New Zealand's South Island, it was a little reminder of home.

ROEHAMPTON HOSPITAL

It soon became apparent that wounded soldiers most likely to survive in World War One were those hit in legs or arms. In the days before antibiotics, the bad conditions in the front line meant that a quick amputation was the best way to save life.

Hundreds of amputees began to arrive back in England from France, Gallipoli and the Middle East. Large numbers of artificial limbs were urgently needed.

By August 1916, after just two years of war, Queen Mary's Hospital for the Limbless at Roehampton had supplied 800 artificial limbs with 1,900 waiting for a fitting. At war's end 11,000 had been treated.

After arriving back in London on April 21 from his trip to Scotland, Birmingham and Liverpool, Ernie headed to Roehampton Hospital.

Many visits were made for fittings and June 29 saw him admitted as an outpatient. Next day his diary read: 'Tried arm on and took it away. Too damn sore to wear.' That night he consoled himself with a visit to Middlesex Theatre.

He was out to Roehampton almost every second day until the middle of July just trying to get the fitting right.

At Roehampton and wearing his lemon squeezer hat, Ernie stands centre in the second row from the back, alongside the nurse.

SERPENTINE

Wednesday May 24: 'Round Hyde Park and had a row on the Serpentine'. So read an entry in Ernie Young's diary on that late spring day in 1916.

An article in a 1913 Oamaru newspaper told how for most New Zealanders and Australians it was strange to see winter ice on the Serpentine. For Ernie, a man from Otago wandering Hyde Park two winters later, it would have been no novelty. It would perhaps have been more of a surprise in the summer to see people swimming in the lake, but only allowed before 8.30am in the morning. According to the visiting newspaper man the water was not particularly clean — flecked with tiny soot balls and dust. That did not seem to worry the hundreds of Londoners who enjoyed an outdoor swim early on a Saturday morning.

The newspaper noted: 'A row in a light skiff on the Serpentine has its attractive side, even though for someone from 'down under' accustomed to larger spaces, it has the feeling of playing at boating around a toy lake'.

QUEEN MARY AND PRINCESS ALEXANDRA

OFTEN SEEN TOGETHER, Princess Alexandra of Teck and Queen Mary, consort of King George both worked hard for Britain's war effort. Ernie did not record when and where this picture was taken, but it would appear to have been in palace grounds.

Queen Mary instituted a reign of wartime austerity at Buckingham Palace and even rationed food.

Although she found it an emotional strain there were many visits to wounded and sick soldiers. In 1917 she visited the Western Front with the King to inspect army hospitals.

In March 1916 the King and Queen entertained convalescing soldiers over three days at the palace. One thousand veterans each day, including many Anzacs, were invited to afternoon tea and a concert, and it is then Ernie probably captured this shot.

In another huge outing 6,000 Anzac soldiers were entertained. London taxis and private cars were offered to take the veterans to afternoon tea in Windsor Park.

Vast quantities of food were donated by London firms including fruit cake from Selfridges along with sandwiches, grapes, apples, cups of tea, coffee and plenty of cigarettes.

During the afternoon Princess Alexandra, her sister Princess Mary and Princess Christian walked around the marquees to speak with the soldiers.

GARDEN PARTY

By November 1918, the last month of World War One, it was recorded that more than one thousand English homes were thrown open for the entertainment and recuperation of New Zealand, Australian and other Dominion soldiers.

The New Zealand War Contingent Association was formed at the start of the war to look after New Zealand soldiers on leave or in hospital in England. The Association arranged amusements for them, trips out, and very often they were made house guests of hosts in London, Scotland and in the provinces.

The sick and wounded troops from 'down under' had been welcomed from Gallipoli as early as 1915 and lauded as the 'Anzacs'. Ernie was one of them. He appears to have mostly preferred to stay in London to see all the sights he had heard about all his life.

Places such as Tower of London, Petticoat Lane, Leicester Square and Buckingham Palace. He enjoyed visits to the stage shows and the movie theatres but also was keen to visit English hosts when the chance came.

Garden parties were another favourite pastime for Ernie and his mates. Despite their difficulties the men were full of life and fun.

In this photo Ernie, third from left, has carefully posed with his mate to make it appear as if they had only one arm, three legs and one hand to share between them.

It was the spirit and attitude that Ernie kept all his life.

THAMES

ERNIE SEEMS HAPPY and relaxed at this garden party given for him and some of his Anzac friends by two English hostesses at their London mansion garden.

The caption under this photo in Ernie's album simply reads 'Thames'. The food and drink on the table in the background has been dealt with by the invited soldiers. A dog, probably the family pet, is hoping for leftovers.

Another photo snapped at the party shows two soldiers a little self consciously holding a bunch of flowers each, the bouquets to be presented to the ladies as a 'thank you'.

A story in the Poverty Bay Herald of March 7, 1916: 'New Zealanders have reason to feel grateful for the solicitude shown to their soldier boys, some five thousand of whom, so far, have been invalided to England. People of all classes have vied with one another in tendering hospitality and kindness to these lads, many of them maimed on the battlefield, many wasted with disease

ISLEWORTH ON THAMES

contracted upon the inhospitable shores of Gallipoli, many lonely and homesick so many thousands of miles away from home'.

Ernie was one New Zealand soldier that certainly enjoyed the hospitality and kindness of the English people.

Always a keen sportsman, Ernie did not let losing his right arm discourage him. On sick leave he wrote: 'To garden party at Isleworth in afternoon. Won prize at golf'.

As large numbers of wounded and sick soldiers arrived back in England in 1915 an old disused school in Isleworth was taken over as a temporary hospital for them. Three hundred beds were accommodated in two wings. During the war the hospital looked after 4,989 soldiers and remarkably, only one patient ever died there.

Anzac soldiers were hosted in many of the grand houses all over London. Ernie's golfing garden party photo was probably taken at the hospital or perhaps at one of Isleworth's great old Georgian mansions.

ROTTEN ROW

For New Zealanders sightseeing in London, a visit to Rotten Row was a must.

Built in 1690 as a Royal carriage way for King William II, it included a sandy track alongside especially designed for the upper classes to ride their horses. Named 'Route de Roi', French for King's Road, it was eventually corrupted to Rotten Row. For Anzacs it was the place to go for a chance to see royalty, politicians or some other famous person riding past.

In 1919 a returned soldier told how he had spent an hour in Hyde Park and thought that it was 'the most beautiful park he had ever sat in after touring the world'.

He described Rotten Row as 'a straight mile course of sandy soil kept constantly watered.'

At afternoon tea and on their best behaviour, New Zealand soldiers came from many differing backgrounds. When they joined the army these men were clerks or carpenters, farmers or bushmen, lawyers or labourers. Few would ever have imagined that one day they would be taking tea at a table set with flowers in an English garden, waited on by English ladies with some association with New Zealand, and by New Zealanders living in England.

Most of the care for the

AFTERNOON TEA

wounded and sick colonial boys was organised by the New Zealand War Contingent Association set up in England by New Zealand High Commissioner Sir Thomas McKenzie together with former New Zealand Governor General Lord Plunket.

The War Contingent report of 1916 told how the voluntary workers were 'devoting themselves day by day to arduous tasks with remarkable self sacrifice and patriotism. Thus are found the daughter of Lord Plunket and other young ladies classed as kitchen helpers, performing drudgeries of housework or clerical duties'.

Lord Plunket wrote: 'One of the bright spots of the war has been the splendid way in which our women have risen to the occasion and shown that no work is too hard for them, no duties too menial, no self sacrifice too great'.

Some of those ladies are seen in the background at this afternoon tea.

The empty chair in the foreground probably belongs to photographer Ernie Young.

ROEHAMPTON

This may be the last photo of Ernie with some of the nurses and his fellow patients before they left Roehampton Hospital. Ernie is still in uniform standing in the back row between two nurses.

His diary noted on February 28, 1916: 'Left Roehampton for three months furlough pending completion of arm'.

Mid-March he was away to Scotland, meeting up with his friends in Glasgow and visiting Edinburgh, Manchester, Birmingham and Liverpool before heading back to London in time for the very first Anzac Day commemoration on April 25. He witnessed a Zeppelin raid on the city that night with a searchlight finding the intruder and shells bursting around it. He watched a procession along Whitehall to Westminster Abbey and noted meeting Lieutenant General Sir William Birdwood, a senior officer in Britain's pre-1914 Indian Army, who commanded the Australian and New Zealand forces when they assembled in Egypt.

In July Ernie was back at Roehampton for a final fitting of his arm. It was an accessory that he never ever found very helpful.

GOING HOME:
LEAVING FOR NEW ZEALAND

GOING HOME! THE great day came for Ernie on August 12.

His laconic diary entry: 'Went before medical board. Leaving tomorrow to catch Willochra.

August 11: 'Left Hornchurch Camp 8.30am, Romford 9am Paddington 11.30am for Newport, arriving at boat 3.30pm embarked'. The New Zealand Steamship company vessel left Newport at 6 o'clock the next morning. It was just nine days short of one year since Ernie was hit on Gallipoli.

In an intriguing footnote to Ernie's sojourn in Britain was a diary entry which simply noted at one point: 'Afternoon tea at Lady and Sir Ian Hamilton's.' As a former bodyguard to the general, and apparently allowed to carry a forbidden camera, that social occasion speaks volumes. It has never been elaborated upon in the years that have passed since then.

Whether any other members of the bodyguard in the United Kingdom at the time, or he alone was invited, Ernie never explained.

HOMEWARD BOUND

It was Saturday August 12, 1916 and Ernie Young was heading home aboard the Willochra. On board were about 170 soldiers including a group of nurses, five returning wives of officers and soldiers and one civilian passenger.

'Left Newport 6 o'clock. Destroyer 70 escorting. Willochra very empty and rolling a lot. Breezy going down the Bristol Channel'.

It was not a good start for the wounded and sick soldiers, but next day was a little better for them. 'Fine weather but boat still rolls and heaves a lot. Church parade at 11 o'clock. Destroyer still cutting around us'. On Monday morning when the escort left them Ernie wrote: 'Fine weather, put on dormitory sergeant for voyage'. He was also given another job on a sergeant's mess committee.

It would keep him busy all the way home with those two responsibilities, printing his photos, concerts, continuous competitions and games held on the ship.

As they headed south through the Bay of Biscay Ernie noticed the conditions improving: 'Sea fairly calm but boat rolling a good bit' he noted in his diary.

There was drama once when they were 'held up by cruiser HMS Kent'.

Ernie did not explain, but all on board would not have appreciated any hold ups.

WILLOCHRA'S GUN

THERE WERE MORE hold ups for the returning veterans when one of the ship's steam pipes burst. A diary entry reads: 'Steam pipe burst and boat stopped for three hours'.

He never commented but it would have been a nervous wait for the service men and women while the engine room crew was making repairs. They were only four days out from England and German U-boats were lurking.

But there were distractions. A concert was held on the boat deck that night and next day there was a hard to imagine cricket match between the officers and sergeants. The weather was kind and stayed fine for two more days. 'We passed two or three ships, and concert held aft'.

August 20: Another stop was made at Dakar, a city on the very western point of the African continent. 'We arrived at Dakar at 9 o'clock, stopped two hours to take gun off. Very funny watching natives diving for pennies'. That night when they sailed from Dakar Ernie wrote, 'Rough tonight'.

Next day was even worse. 'Very rough today, raining and blowing hard.' It was August 21. Exactly one year had passed since the attack on Hill 60, the last big battle at Gallipoli and the day that he lost an arm.

CAPETOWN

ON FRIDAY, SEPTEMBER 1, Willochra arrived at Capetown. For the New Zealanders there were two full days of shore leave to enjoy. S S Ulimaroa was also in port with a load of New Zealand soldiers, reinforcements heading for Europe. The two ships between them ran a shuttle service taking troops to the war and bringing back the wounded and sick.

Ernie (centre) and his mates, looking spruce in shining boots and neat uniform, were off on leave on the first day until 11pm. They started with a 'motor trip around Table Mountain' and later — 'At the Opera House at night'.

Saturday morning saw them wandering the shops of Cape Town maybe with souvenirs in mind. In the afternoon the sightseers went 'to the gardens in the afternoon. Listened to band on the pier'.

Sunday at 10 o'clock they were off again and heading into almost a week of bad weather. He noted that day on leaving port, 'Very rough outside.' And next day 'Very rough, high sea running, boat rolls a lot.' It went on for days.

Tuesday: 'Still very rough and rolling. Very cold'.

They were probably sailing more to the south as a safety precaution. Because of his artificial limb Ernie and the other amputees were possibly not too comfortable moving around in those conditions.

NURSES ON BOARD

A TEAM OF nurses was aboard the Willochra and in the photo one of them gets a little help while trying on her lifebelt.

Altogether in 1916 there were 204 nurses under the command of the New Zealand Forces and several were decorated for their work in hospitals, on hospital ships, and at the front.

Aboard was Sister G M Lewis who had been wounded in the trenches while serving in Serbia and Belgium and had been decorated personally by King Peter of Serbia for her rescue work.

In October 1915, 10 New Zealand nurses and 22 male medical staff drowned while travelling to Salonika. They were staff from New Zealand No.1 Stationary Hospital working in Egypt and were aboard ammunition ship Marquette when she was torpedoed in the Aegean Sea. Too late it was realised that nurses should never have been aboard an ammunitions carrier.

CROSSING THE EQUATOR

MOST OF THOSE aboard Willochra had crossed the equator on their way to war in 1914. That wasn't going to stop them enjoying the fun a second time, dressing up and dealing with King Neptune.

Weather stayed fine for a few days and Ernie entered in his diary: 'Games going on, printing photos, sports held this afternoon, very good'.

Concerts were often held on deck. In typical indomitable high spirits the men held unusual competitions, enjoying themselves and helping pass the time. An always athletic Ernie won first prize for fastest 'dressing for one armed men'. There were strange sights to see from the deck: 'Clear and cold, with a lot of whales about' he wrote on August 30 as the passage home took them further into the safety of the southern ocean. A few days previously he had written: 'Lights out at eight o'clock tonight. We are off German West Africa'. Again the next night it was, 'All lights out'.

Although they were on the way to peaceful New Zealand, the war still dominated their lives.

HOME AGAIN

At last they were on the final leg to home. After leaving Cape Town Ernie and his mates survived three days and nights of very rough and cold weather. On the fourth day he thought it had quietened down a little but 'the men were shifted down below into the cabins'. It was good enough though to hold the final of the cricket matches.

On Friday September 8 a quoits match was played with a concert the next night and a prize giving.

Within a couple of days the bad weather came back Ernie noted: 'Wet day and heaving sea running'. His frustration was perhaps starting to show when he started to record the daily totals of miles covered. The ship was averaging about 300 miles a day but the weather was still bleak, so much so that unusually for him, Ernie gave in just a little. September 18: 'Raining and hailing. Very cold. In bunk nearly all of day'.

September 19: 'Very cold. Sleet hail and snow falling'. But they were still in the army and he remembered that with two words in his diary — 'Kit inspection'.

The cold, snow and rain went on for a few more days, causing

cancellation of the last sports day. That night though they held a fancy dress, book and song guessing competition and Ernie 'landed third prize'.

ERNIE WITH HIS DOG

Friday September 22, 1916 was a good day for the homecoming war veterans on the Willochra. Ernie took photos, it was fine, there was a good wind blowing, ship board sports were continuing, they had covered 328 sea miles and there was the presentation of prizes.

Next day made it seem as if they were almost there. 'Fine morning, passed along coast of Tasmania at eight o'clock this morning'.

Four days later he could write: 'Passed Puysegur Point at eight o'clock in the morning.' Their first sight of New Zealand was the very bottom south-western corner of the South Island. Now was the time for last farewells and Ernie wrote: 'Final concert tonight and supper'.

On September 28 they were home: 'Arrived at the Heads 2 o'clock this morning, reached Port Chalmers at 8 o'clock'.

But it was a remarkably low key arrival with no emotion, drama, or brass bands.

Ernie entered the bare facts in his diary: 'Got through medical board and away home about 11 o'clock'.

He had been gone two weeks short of two years, had experienced many adventures, enjoyed good times and suffered bad times.

ABOUT THE AUTHOR

BRIAN LIVED HIS entire life in Dargaville, New Zealand but had a never-ending curiosity about the world, a special interest in local history, the history of both World Wars and in particular the role of the New Zealand Defence Forces in them, about all different cultures and all of mankind.

He was widely regarded as a true gentleman and historian and once retired he pursued his love of writing and research with an extremely popular regular column for a local newspaper. This book *Gallipoli: A Soldier's Story* is the culmination of a lifetime of quiet ambition to be a published author.

www.ingramcontent.com/pod-product-compliance
Lightning Source LLC
Chambersburg PA
CBHW070338120526
44590CB00017B/2935